JAE BROWN

The 7 Guaranteed Steps to Change the World

Contents

Foreword

In the early 2010s, I was on a path that would shape not only my career but also contribute to a lasting impact on global public health and emergency preparedness. It all began with my role at the Centers for Disease Control and Prevention (CDC) as part of the Emergency Operations Center (EOC), where I was responsible for coordinating responses to public health emergencies. My work caught the attention of key leaders, including the Deputy Director of my division, who strongly recommended me for a newly created position that would catapult me into a pivotal role in safeguarding national security: Emergency Management Coordinator for the CDC's Division of Select Agents and Toxins (DSAT).

This position was created out of necessity. The Bush-Cheney Administration identified one of the most significant threats to national security was the lack of a coordinated emergency response plan for laboratories housing the world's most dangerous agents and toxins. With over 300 labs, each having its own individual incident response plan, there was no cohesive strategy. It was an untenable situation. As a result, my task was to develop a comprehensive national plan to unify emergency responses across all laboratories in the event of a natural disaster or other critical incidents.

The task was enormous, but so was my passion for emergency management—a passion I had discovered during my time in the Army National Guard, working part-time on emergency response while building my career. That passion drove me to create something that would make a difference. I set out to find a solution, starting with assembling a team of experts, advocates, and supporters who shared my vision. I evaluated the gaps in the existing response systems and built a framework that could integrate seamlessly into DSAT's regulatory responsibilities. The plan I wrote didn't just sit on a shelf;

it reached the desk of the President of the United States for signature and approval.

Once approved, the real work began. I was tasked with implementing the plan across the country, training laboratory personnel, and attending conferences to ensure the plan was understood and adopted. The implementation was so effective that the U.S. Department of Health and Human Services (HHS), Under Secretary for Emergency Management, praised our efforts during a call with world leaders in public health. I still remember the words my Division Director relayed to me: "If you want to know how to develop and implement a national emergency management plan, you should talk to my subject matter expert down at the CDC's DSAT." Those words echoed far beyond that call—they opened the door for me to become an international consultant.

The plan that I had written in my office in Atlanta was soon being implemented globally. I helped CDC Europe, CDC China, and various other nations develop and adapt the framework. Today, it protects over two billion people worldwide. My story, however, is not unique. It follows a path that anyone can take. A path rooted in the seven guaranteed steps that, when followed with intention and purpose, can change the world.

Those seven steps are what this book is about:

1. Find a Passion: For me, it was emergency management, discovered while working with the Army National Guard and cemented during my time at the CDC.
2. Build a Team: I created a network of advocates who believed in my vision and supported my career trajectory, helping me transition from an intern to a full-time emergency manager.
3. Evaluate the Gaps and Seams of the Team: By assessing the existing skills of my team I found the right group of people who would advocate for me and parlay their belief in me into an opportunity at DSAT.
4. Create a Plan: The national response plan I developed was the cornerstone of my work and the framework that would protect millions.
5. Execute the Plan: Once approved, I implemented it through training, conferences, and continuous oversight.

6. Evaluate the Ups and Downs of the Plan: As the plan rolled out, I continually assessed its effectiveness, made necessary adjustments, and integrated feedback.
7. Do It All Over Again: Every success brought new opportunities to repeat the process on a global scale, adapting the plan for different nations and environments.

These steps aren't just a road map for my journey—they're universal principles that anyone can apply to make an impact. Ordinary people, when following these steps with intention, can achieve extraordinary things. This book will guide you through each of these steps and share the stories of others who, knowingly or unknowingly, have followed this process to create meaningful change in their lives and the world around them.

The seven guaranteed steps to change the world are more than just steps—they are the foundation for becoming a change-maker. Whether your passion is in public health, business, education, or community service, these principles apply universally. By the time you finish this book, you will not only understand how to follow these steps but also how to become part of the movement that is changing the world, one person and one plan at a time.

1

Find Your Passion

Your passion, true passion will be like the roots in Aaron Weaver's "Roots of a Tree". Your passion will be what grounds you. A true passion will produce branches, leaves, and eventually fruit. A passion provides the base to change the world. Everything begins with passion. The journey Jay Bailey, CEO of the Russell Innovation Center for Entrepreneurs (RICE), shared during his TEDWomen 2023 speech, beautifully aligns with this idea. His story is a prevailing testament to how excitement, combined with self-belief and charge, can produce remarkable results for an entire community. In four years RICE has developed a support structure for over 360 entrepreneurs who have created over 1500 jobs. Annually they touch over 10,000 people through their network of partners and stakeholders and have generated over 450 million dollars of new economic activity. They've established the world's largest organization supporting African American entrepreneurs and have formed a space where they feel like their ideas matter and have the freedom to believe.

Action Step: Ask yourself, "What breaks my heart or ignites my soul?" Whether it's environmental protection, educational reform, or even a technological innovation, your passion is where you must begin. Without it, the world will remain unchanged.

Discover what excites, terrifies, or moves you deeply. Passion is not only about what you love—it's about what compels you to act and what you can't ignore.

1. Reflect on Your Interests and Talents

Jay Bailey's journey toward discovering his passion began early in life. In his speech, Bailey shares how, as a child, he was always enterprising—whether making Popsicle to sell or charging neighborhood kids 50 cents to see a WWE style event in his backyard. Though considered gifted as a child, Bailey was a self-proclaimed poor student who despised school. Yet, he flourished in entrepreneurial ventures that would become the key to his future."

The at the age of eleven he had a conversation with his barber, who owned not just one shop, but several. For the first time, Bailey heard the word "entrepreneur," and in that moment, everything clicked for him. He realized that entrepreneurship aligned with his natural skills, and this understanding fueled his passion for business.

Ask Yourself:

- What activities do you lose track of time doing?
- What subjects or topics do you read about or research for fun?
- What skills or talents do you enjoy using or would like to improve?
- **Example:** If you love spending time outdoors and feel invigorated by nature, you might be passionate about environmental conservation.

Action Step: Make a list of hobbies, interests, or activities that make you feel fulfilled or energized. Reflect on how these could connect to a larger cause or issue.

2. Examine What Makes You Feel Empathy or Anger

Bailey's passion for entrepreneurship is deeply tied to his understanding of the challenges faced by black and underserved communities. He speaks about the invisible barriers that keep so many brilliant ideas from ever reaching the marketplace because those individuals do not believe they belong. This inequity ignites a fire in him, driving his work at RICE, where he has created a space for black entrepreneurs to thrive by providing access, opportunity, and exposure. Often, strong emotional reactions like empathy or anger are indicators of what you deeply care about. Bailey paid attention to what stirred him emotionally. His belief that the only difference between the "north side" and the "south side" of the tracks is opportunity, not ability, has fueled his mission to support entrepreneurs who have historically been excluded from traditional avenues of success.

Ask Yourself:

- What global or local issues make you feel a strong emotional response?
- What news stories or causes make you want to take action?
- What injustice or inequality do you feel compelled to solve?
- **Example:** If stories of poverty or homelessness move you, you might be passionate about social justice or affordable housing.

Action Step: Reflect on the last time you felt deeply moved by a cause or issue. Consider what specific elements of that issue resonate with you and how you could get involved in addressing it.

3. Reflect on Your Childhood Interests

Sometimes, your passions are rooted in childhood interests or dreams. Jay reflected on his story of selling Popsicle. Reconnecting with early passions can help uncover what you truly care about today. Reconnecting with these childhood interests helped him realize that he was always meant to be an entrepreneur, even if he didn't have a name for it at the time.

Ask Yourself:

- What did you love to do or learn about as a child?
- What activities or causes did you dream of being part of when you were younger?
- **Example:** If you loved building things with your hands as a child, you may find passion in engineering, design, or sustainable architecture.

Action Step: Write down some of your favorite childhood activities, interests, or aspirations. Think about how they might connect with current passions or issues.

4. Explore and Experiment

"There is no such thing as a failed experiment, only experiments with unexpected outcomes..." (R. Buckminster Fuller). No one is born know their passion and how to utilize that passion to benefit the world. Actively exploring and experimenting with activities around your passions allows you to better understand yourself. Don't be afraid to try new things, volunteer, or take up new hobbies to see what truly resonates.

Ask Yourself:

- What new activities or causes could you try that align with your interests?
- Are there volunteer opportunities or events you could participate in to explore different causes?
- **Example:** If you're interested in education but haven't had direct experience, you could volunteer at a local school or mentor youth to see if this cause excites you.

Action Step: Take action by trying something new—whether it's volunteering for a cause, attending a workshop, or joining a club. Give yourself permission to experiment and see what truly sparks passion.

5. Pay Attention to What Drains You or Excites You at Work

Once Jay Bailey understood what an entrepreneur was, he felt that his life "started to make sense". His passion brought excitement and purpose to his life. Maybe your current job can offer clues about your passions. Which tasks energize you and which drain you? The parts of your job that excite you could point to a deeper passion, while those that drain you may indicate what you want to avoid. For Jay, it wasn't just the act of running businesses but empowering others to do the same that brought him fulfillment.

Ask Yourself:

- What parts of my work bring me the most joy or fulfillment?
- What activities make me feel drained or disengaged?
- **Example:** If mentoring younger colleagues excites you while sitting in meetings drains you, you might have a passion for education, coaching, or personal development.

Action Step: Reflect on your workday and write down tasks that energize and fulfill you. Consider how these tasks align with potential passions or larger causes you care about.

6. Consider the Causes or Conversations You Can't Stop Thinking About

Think about the conversations or causes that continually surface in your mind. You know the ones that come up even when you're not actively trying to think about them. These persistent reflections just might be pointing to something deeply significant to you, revealing an underlying passion. When a topic continually catches your attention, it's a strong indicator that it's more than just a passing curiosity. It's a cause or idea that reverberates with your central values and might be worth exploring further.

Ask Yourself:

- What topics come up repeatedly in my conversations?
- What issues do I find myself frequently thinking or talking about with friends and family?
- **Example:** If you often find yourself discussing climate change or sustainable living, your passion may lie in environmental advocacy.

Action Step: Reflect on the conversations you have most often with people close to you. Identify recurring themes or topics that naturally come up and how they might connect to a deeper passion.

7. Identify Role Models or People Who Inspire You

Bailey didn't come from a background of business owners. His understanding of entrepreneurship grew over time through experience and exposure. Who are the people you admire most? Doesn't matter if they are public figures, family members, or colleagues. What are the qualities, causes, or actions that inspire you in others? Allow those thoughts to give you insight into your own values and passions.

Jay's passion for helping others succeed also evolved as he grew, and he continually experimented with ways to empower marginalized communities through entrepreneurship. In his speech he expressed how RICE has created a space rooted in belonging and empowerment, offering black entrepreneurs the tools and resources they need to succeed.

Ask Yourself:

- Who are the people I admire most, and why do they inspire me?
- What causes or actions do my role models champion that resonate with me?
- **Example:** If you admire activists like Malala Yousafzai or Greta Thunberg, your passion might align with education for girls or environmental advocacy.

Action Step: Make a list of people who inspire you and the causes they champion. Consider how those causes might align with your own values and potential passions.

8.Consider What You Would Do If Money Weren't an Issue

Cliche's are cliches for a reason. So let's explore this common one. Imagine a life where financial limitations no longer exist—where bills, savings, and budgets are no longer a concern. Where and what would you dedicate your time to? This cliche allows you to focus on what brings you joy, fulfillment, or purpose. With practicality out of the picture, you can paint a vision of the passions and pursuits that truly matter to you. What actually drives you at a core level?

Ask Yourself:

- If I didn't have to work for money, what would I spend my time doing?
- What causes or activities would I pursue with full freedom?
- **Example:** If you would spend your time volunteering with wildlife conservation efforts, your passion might lie in animal welfare or environmental protection.

Action Step: Spend time imagining your ideal day or week if you didn't have to worry about money. Write down the activities you would focus on and reflect on how they could translate into meaningful work or causes.

9. Pay Attention to Your Natural Curiosity

When exploring your natural curiosities take note. You are getting a glimpse into your passions. That sense of wonder, excitement for knowledge and wondering how you can be a part of the solution can be the roots to a great plan for changing the world.

Ask Yourself:

- What subjects do I often research or read about in my spare time?
- What areas of life do I feel curious to explore more deeply?
- **Example:** If you're always curious about health and wellness, you might be passionate about promoting holistic health or public health education.

Action Step: Reflect on what you spend your time researching, learning, or exploring on your own. Consider how your curiosity might point to causes or fields you care about.

10. Seek Feedback from Friends and Family

Do you pay attention to what people observe about your actions or thoughts. It's those people closest to you that can offer insights into your passions that you may not see yourself. Ask friends, family, or colleagues what they consider you to be most passionate about, centered on their reflections.

Ask Them:

- What do you think I'm most passionate about?
- What topics or causes do you see me getting excited about?
- **Example:** Your friends might point out that you always light up when talking about helping others, indicating a passion for community service or mentoring.

Action Step: Reach out to a few trusted people in your life and ask them for feedback on what they see as your passions. Use their insights to gain clarity on your own feelings.

Conclusion: Follow Your Passion's Path

Discovering your passion is an ongoing journey, not a one-time decision. Jay

Bailey's journey is a living example of what it means to find your passion. His passion for entrepreneurship and for uplifting others was ignited by a combination of early experiences, powerful role models, and a deep empathy for those who are often overlooked. For Bailey, passion wasn't just about business—it was about using his talent to create opportunities for others and to make a lasting impact on his community. Now it's your turn!

2

Build a Team

Your passion is something that is internal within you. As John Donne famously expresses in his works "No Man is an Island" we are all interconnected. So changing the world is never and should never be a solo venture. With your passion identified, forming a team becomes essential. No one can single-handedly bring about lasting change. Humility is understanding you are not the source of all good ideas. A diverse and united team becomes the key to scaling your mission. Don't be daunted by the task of building a large and diverse team. A team can start with you and one other person, doing small things that will eventually attract others to your cause. Stewart Butterfield began his first business with just one other person, proving that impactful ventures can start small. Stewart Butterfield's path to building Slack embodies several of the essential principles outlined in this chapter. His experience reflects how gathering the right team and leveraging complementary skills were essential to transforming failure into a billion-dollar success story.

Action Step: Identify those who share your passion and possess complementary skills. Begin with friends, colleagues, mentors, or even online networks. Surround yourself with people who not only believe in your cause but who will push you to be better.

How to Gather Support for Your World-Changing Mission

Gathering support for your mission is like a muscle, it gets stronger the more you exercise it. Support comes in many forms—financial, emotional, logistical, or in the form of people who help spread your message..

1. Start with Your Inner Circle

After the failure of Steve's earlier projects, such as his attempt to create a multiplayer online game, Butterfield realized the need for a team that shared his passion but also brought different skills to the table. In the early stages, Stewart recruited individuals from his inner circle, including Jason Klassen and Cal Henderson, who had already worked with him on prior ventures. This was Butterfield's first step in rallying a core group around his vision, even when the original mission seemed to be failing.

The best way to find the first people to rally around your cause is to look at those closest to you—friends, family, and colleagues. They may not all be passionate about your specific mission, but they are more likely to help you simply because they care about you. Share your vision with them, explain why it matters, and ask them to be involved in some way. Even if they can't commit much time, they can offer valuable encouragement, feedback, and even introductions to others who may be able to help.

Action Step: Host a small gathering or have one-on-one conversations with people in your inner circle. Present your idea passionately and ask them to get involved, whether by providing feedback, offering resources, or connecting you with people in their network.

2. Leverage Social Media and Online Communities

Early in Slack's development the company utilized online networks and social media to gather support and momentum. This engagement provided a pivotal turning point in the development of the company. Early users provided feedback that allowed Butterfield and his team to iteratively improve Slack until it became a more polished, user-friendly application.

In today's world, social media is a powerful tool for gathering support. Your immediate network is much more than your church, classmates and friends. Your reach can now be people far beyond your immediate network. A well-constructed presence on various platforms is your gateway to targeted audiences and like-minded communities. Whether it's Facebook, Instagram, LinkedIn, Twitter, or niche forums, share your mission in compelling and authentic ways. Show people why they should care about your cause and how they can be a part of the change.

Engage with like-minded communities and participate in conversations related to your passion. When people see your sincerity and the value of your mission, they are more likely to support it.

Action Step: Create dedicated social media pages for your cause and post regular updates, stories, and actionable ways for people to get involved. Use hashtags and keywords to reach a wider audience and engage directly with followers by responding to their questions and comments.

3. Build Strategic Partnerships

One of the most effective ways to gather support is by building partnerships with organizations or individuals who share a similar mission. The shift from a game development company to Slack came about because of Butterfield's ability to pivot and his team's willingness to adapt. His partnership with investors such as Andreessen Horowitz initially faced challenges, as they were skeptical about the company's direction. However, Stewart's ability to foster relationships with key investors led to continued support despite initial doubts about the viability of Slack as a product. This reflects the principle of finding strategic partners who may not fully understand your mission initially but can provide crucial resources once they see potential.

Whether formal or informal, partnerships fostered on mutual benefits will amplify your reach, lend credibility to your cause, and provide access to resources you might not have on your own.

Action Step: Research organizations that align with your mission. Send them a clear and concise pitch explaining how your cause complements theirs and how a partnership would create a win-win situation. Be sure to follow up after initial outreach.

4. Tell Compelling Stories

Emotional connections tend to move people to action. A powerful story is one of the most powerful ways to gather support because it allows you to create a personal, emotional connection with your audience. Put a picture in someone's head about how your mission will have an impact on people. Your story doesn't have to be personal, it just needs to show how action will benefit the targeted audience. When people understand how your work can change lives, they're more likely to support it. Make them a part of something that creates tangible, meaningful change.

Action Step: Craft a series of stories that show the real-life impact of your mission. Use these stories in speeches, social media posts, blogs, and conversations to evoke empathy and inspire people to take action.

5. Create an Opportunity for Others to Get Involved

You have found your passion, like-minded people and a compelling story. You have the attention of potential team members. The best way to keep them engaged is to find a way for them to be involved. Be sure to make it easy for people to get involved in your mission. Start with straight forward requests like volunteering time, donating money, spreading the word, or offering their expertise. These initial steps need to be clear and actionable ways for them to help. This is your first leadership challenge to changing the world. While you may not have a clear actional plan, you should have a direction or path to get to that actionable plan.

Action Step: Create a clear "call to action" that outlines exactly how people can support your mission. For example, include links to donate, sign-up sheets for volunteers, or toolkits for spreading the word on social media.

6. Provide Tangible Results

Always remember people want to know how their support is making a difference. Like you, they want to make tangible changes to the world around them. Provide regular updates on the impact of your mission by sharing results. Success stories are the most powerful examples. However, progress updates and statistics also allows your supporters to see how their contributions are making the world a better place. These actions will keep your team invested.

Action Step: Create periodic progress reports or infographics that highlight key achievements, milestones, and how supporters have played a role in the mission. Send these updates via email, post them on social media, or present them at community meetings. Don't forget the personal touch also, handwritten notes, private conversations and individually targeted gifts of appreciation will build devotion not only to the cause but to you.

7. Host Events or Workshops

While this can be interpreted as creeping in on other steps in this plan, hosting events can be a great way to recruit for building a team. Simple events like a dinner party can allow you to connect with people in a more personal, engaging way. Community-building workshops and online webinars are other low stress ways to provide opportunities to share your mission with new audiences and strengthen your bond with existing supporters.

During events, make it easy for attendees to take the next step—whether that's donating, volunteering, or spreading the word.

Action Step: Plan a gathering, workshop, or webinar to promote your mission. Invite people who are interested in your cause and use the event to build relationships and offer tangible ways for people to get involved.

8. Stay Consistent and Persistent

Don't give up, support doesn't come overnight. Developing a loyal group of supporters requires consistency and persistence. Continue to share your message regularly and engage with people over time. Often, people are waiting to see if your commitment to the cause is genuine and long-term before they join you.

Consistency is the key to showing this is a true passion vs. a flavor of the month. Persistent messaging, action, and outreach builds trust.

Action Step: Create a long-term engagement plan. Ensure that you're consistently following up with supporters, sharing new updates, and providing ways for people to stay involved over time.

9. Lead by Example

When people see your passion and dedication firsthand, they are much more likely to be inspired and get involved. Mr. Butterfield's ability to lead by example, staying committed to the broader goal of building a successful company even in the face of setbacks, inspired his team to follow suit. A critical aspect of Slack's success was Butterfield's ability to pivot and provide tangible results. His Regular feedback loops and tangible improvements to the platform kept the team focused on delivering a product that worked.

People are naturally drawn to leaders whose actions speak for themselves. Your commitment to the mission should be no less than those who are supporting you. Roll up your sleeves and make it happen.

Action Step: Be visible and involved in every aspect of your mission. Attend events, engage with supporters, and be hands-on with the work. Show your followers that you are a leader who walks the talk.

Conclusion: Building a Movement, One Supporter at a Time

There are plenty of people who want to be part of something bigger than themselves, to have the opportunity to contribute to a cause that makes a real difference. Find your team through building relationships, sharing a compelling vision, and demonstrating tangible results. Stewart Butterfield's creation of Slack is a perfect example of building a team to achieve a shared vision. After the failure of his online game, Stewart rallied his close circle, including Jason Klassen and Cal Henderson, who brought diverse skills that complemented his leadership. Together, they pivoted from the game to develop Slack, leveraging Cal's programming expertise to build the app. Despite early investor skepticism, Butterfield's strategic partnerships and persistence kept the company moving forward. He engaged early users to refine Slack through feedback, aligning with his goal to provide a tool that solved real-world communication problems. By adapting, delivering tangible results, and leading with resilience, Stewart and his team transformed what started as a failed gaming venture into a billion-dollar platform. His ability to pivot and utilize the strengths of his team shows how a united group can turn setbacks into success while changing how businesses communicate.

3

Evaluate the Gaps and Seams of Your Team

Once your team is assembled, it's time to take a clear, honest look at where the gaps lie. Even the most passionate, talented group of people has areas that need development. Perhaps your team lacks a certain technical skill, experience in a particular field, or resources like funding or connections.

The 1971-72 Los Angeles Lakers were put together to change the landscape of the NBA. Armed with three of the top four all time scorers on the NBA scoring list and a new coach, they were ready to become in real life what they were on paper. Despite their individual brilliance, the team had struggled in their previous attempts at securing an NBA title, and they faced several challenges that needed to be addressed if they were to break through. The journey of this Lakers team to their long-awaited championship mirrors the action steps outlined in Chapter 3 of *The 7 Guaranteed Steps to Change the World*.

Action Step: Start by evaluating your team's strengths and weaknesses. Pinpoint the areas where expertise is lacking and assess which skills or resources you still need. Create a list and seek solutions, whether that's further training, adding new members, or partnering with external experts.

Evaluating gaps and seams on a team that's built to change the world is essential to maximizing efficiency, fostering innovation, and ensuring long-term success. Here's how you can effectively assess these areas:

1. Evaluate Skills and Expertise

Begin by analyzing the skills and expertise present on your team. Every team member brings unique strengths, but there will also be gaps in knowledge or experience that need to be filled. Despite having elite offensive players, gaps still existed. Bill Sharman, the coach, recognized that while future hall of fame player Wilt Chamberlain was a dominant scorer, the team needed him to focus more on defense and rebounding to better support the fast-paced game. So he pivoted Chamberlain's role to prioritize defense, allowing other team members like Goodrich and McMillian to shine offensively. This team also was one of the most injured teams of that season, Bill Sharman was constantly evaluating how to maximize the team through injuries to stars like Jerry West and Elgin Baylor, Wilt Chamberlain and others.

Action Step: Create a skills matrix for your team. List the core competencies required to achieve your mission (e.g., technical skills, leadership, marketing, fundraising, communication) and identify which members have expertise in each area. Are there crucial skills missing? If so, consider training, outsourcing, or bringing in new team members to fill these gaps.

2. Assess Team Diversity

Diversity of thought, background, and experience is critical for world-changing teams. Homogeneous teams may suffer from groupthink or limited perspectives, missing out on creative solutions or innovation.

The Lakers' success wasn't just about individual talent—it was about having the right mix of roles and perspectives. Bill Sharman understood that the team could no longer rely on an aging Elgin Baylor, so he introduced Jim McMillian, who brought fresh energy and new tactics to the team's forward position. Also, for years, the Lakers was a team that relied on a more conventional, slow-paced game plan. Sharman established a fast-break offense. He realized that Chamberlain's rebounding dominance could be used to create quick outlet passing opportunities guards Jerry West and Gail Goodrich. The speed and agility of the guards would be on full display.

Action Step: Evaluate your team's diversity across multiple dimensions — professional background, culture, gender, age, and perspectives. Ask yourself: Does your team reflect the diversity of the people or problems you're trying to serve? Where might different viewpoints be lacking? Consider adding people with differing experiences to widen your problem-solving approach.

3. Examine Role Clarity

Role clarity became crucial as the Lakers moved deeper into the playoffs. Each player knew exactly what they were supposed to contribute. For example, when Dave DeBusschere of the Knicks played injured, the Lakers capitalized on the confusion in their opponents' lineup. Meanwhile, Los Angeles had established clear communication and defined responsibilities. Jerry West, while struggling with shooting, contributed through playmaking and assists. Chamberlain, despite his usual scoring prowess, focused on defense and rebounding, enabling others to excel in scoring.

Action Step: Review the roles and responsibilities of each team member. Is there any overlap, which could lead to inefficiency? Are there critical functions no one has been assigned to handle? Consider creating clear job descriptions for each role and ensuring team members are accountable for their specific areas.

4. Analyze Communication Patterns

Effective communication is the backbone of any successful team. Poor communication can lead to misunderstandings, missed deadlines, and frustration. Evaluate how your team shares information, handles conflict, and collaborates across tasks. The Lakers' internal communication was also fine-tuned. Players took the lead in establishing internal communications. As the leader of the team Jerry West ensured open lines of communication on and off the court, enabling the team to adapt and respond to changing situations effectively. Through this communication during critical moments, the Lakers ended the season with 69 wins that included their famous 33-game win streak and the playoffs.

Action Step: Observe your team's communication patterns. Are meetings effective and purposeful? Is information being shared openly, or are there silos forming? Encourage regular, open, and transparent communication, and implement tools (such as Slack or project management software) that streamline communication and collaboration.

5. Check Alignment with Mission and Values

The Lakers shared a singular mission: to finally bring a championship to Los Angeles. The last two seasons ended in disappointment, deep runs in the playoffs was not enough. Sharman's leadership reinforced this mission, and any team members not fully aligned, such as the retiring Baylor, either found new roles or stepped aside. As you build your team, make sure their passion and commitment aligns with the mission you're trying to accomplish. Team members who are not fully on board will become distracted and possibly create internal friction while slowing progress.

Action Step: Have candid discussions with your team about their connection to the mission. Do they feel passionate about it? Are their personal values aligned with the team's? If there are misalignments, consider whether team members need a different role, more clarity on the mission, or if they're a long-term fit for the cause.

6. Evaluate Leadership and Decision-Making

Strong leadership is essential for steering the team toward its goals. Consider how decisions are being made, who holds authority, and whether leadership is effectively guiding the team toward its objectives. The leadership transition to Bill Sharman was pivotal. He implemented new conditioning programs, altered the team's playstyle, and shifted the team's mindset from focusing on individual accolades to a collective goal. Bill Sharman's leadership style also allowed for inclusive decision-making. He empowered key players like West and Goodrich while maintaining his leadership control. Unlike the previous coach who was known for being too loose with the players, coach Sharman always maintained authority.

Action Step: Assess the leadership structure. Does the decision-making process allow for input from all relevant team members? Are decisions being made efficiently, or is the team bogged down by indecision or bureaucracy? If needed, refine leadership roles or adjust decision-making processes to promote agility and inclusivity.

7. Review Resource Allocation

A team's success depends not just on the people, but also on how well resources are distributed. This includes financial, technological, and informational resources. The Lakers' journey also highlighted the importance of resource allocation. Chamberlain's focus on defense freed up resources in terms of scoring, allowing guards like West and Goodrich to flourish offensively. Wilt also used other parts of his game in critical moments like in Game 5 in the NBA finals where he almost recorded a quadruple-double. The team's reliance on its key players like Chamberlain and West required managing their physical and mental resources wisely, ensuring they could perform at their best when it mattered most.

Action Step: Evaluate whether each team member has the resources they need to succeed. Are there any areas where the team is under-resourced? This might include technology, data, workspace, or access to mentorship. Identify areas where additional support or resources could accelerate progress.

8. Analyze Team Dynamics and Collaboration

One of the Lakers' strongest assets was their ability to collaborate and work as a cohesive unit. Coach Sharman worked hard to make sure there was a team first mentality. He assured no one player dominated the spotlight. The team's camaraderie, mutual respect, and collaboration were pivotal in their record-breaking season.How well your team works together affects their ability to achieve big results. Poor team dynamics, such as conflict or lack of trust, can slow progress and demoralize members.

Action Step: Pay attention to team interactions. Is there mutual respect, trust, and camaraderie among team members? Are conflicts resolved quickly and respectfully? Consider team-building activities, open communication workshops, or even bringing in a mediator to resolve underlying issues.

9. Look for Burnout or Overload

The Lakers faced significant physical and emotional stress during their record-breaking season. Sharman knew that this would be a factor for this aging team. He saw how they came close but did not have enough to win at the end of the season. To fix this potential problem he focused on conditioning at the beginning of the season and assured each player had sufficient rest to helped prevent burnout. This strategic management of energy ensured that the team was at full strength during the playoffs.Sometimes gaps and seams arise from team members being overextended. Burnout can decrease productivity and creativity, leading to missed opportunities or mistakes.

Action Step: Regularly check in with your team to assess workloads. Are people working long hours without breaks? Are some team members carrying too much of the load while others may not be fully utilized? Adjust workloads to distribute responsibilities more evenly and prevent burnout.

10. Gather Feedback from Outside the Team

Sometimes, it's hard to see your own blind spots. Gathering feedback from stakeholders, customers, or external advisors can reveal gaps that internal evaluation might miss. The Lakers consistently gathered feedback from coaches, analysts, and even opposing teams, adjusting their tactics as they moved deeper into the playoffs.

Action Step: Ask for feedback from people who interact with your team but aren't part of it—clients, advisors, or partners. Their observations may help you see areas of improvement that are otherwise hidden from the internal team.

Conclusion: Closing the Gaps

In the end, the Lakers' 1971-72 season is a testament to the importance of continuously evaluating gaps and seams within a team. Despite starting with stars and talents, the team did not achieve success until they addressed areas of weakness, refined roles, and embraced leadership that could adapt to changing circumstances. Their victory in the NBA Finals wasn't just about superior skills; it was about strategic assessment, adapting to gaps, and creating a cohesive unit from individual strengths.

In your own world-changing team, remember that success lies not in avoiding gaps but in recognizing them as opportunities for growth. By constantly refining roles, evaluating leadership, and ensuring everyone has what they need, your team—like the Lakers—can achieve remarkable results.

4

Develop a Plan

First let me say congratulations! Believe it or not, You are already an admired leader. By reaching this point in your action steps toward changing the world you have found a passion, built a team and evaluated the reach and limits of your team. Developing a plan is no longer a singular endeavor and you should be opening yourself up to ideas. Allow the new excitement around you to help build a plan that will make it easier for you to be an agent of change. Focus on outlining actionable steps that align with your short and long-term goals. This plan should be adaptable, allowing room for growth and flexibility when unexpected challenges arise. In this chapter we will examine the journey of Alcovy High School's band director, Brian Coates. When Mr. Coates started teaching at Covington's Alcovy High, the school was not on the radar for college band directors. Through strategic planning Brian changed that reality and in turn changed the world for his students. The journey of the Alcovy High School Band program exemplifies the power of strategic planning in achieving extraordinary results.

Action Step: Map out your plan. Set short-term and long-term objectives, define key milestones, and assign roles to team members based on their strengths. Ensure that each team member is aware of their responsibilities and the timelines they need to follow. Now here's your guide on how to create a concrete plan.

1. Clarify Your Vision and Mission

Let's start by clearly articulating and stating your *why*. How does working through this passion help you get to the change you want to see in the world? Having a clear vision helps you stay focused and aligned as you move forward. When Brian Coates took over the Alcovy High School band program in 2017, the band lacked the drive and discipline needed for success. Coates had a vision of building a top-tier band program that could compete on a national level. But that was not his why. His why was to provide students with opportunities to earn scholarships for college. This vision was clear and focused: create a band that not only excelled in performance but also changed the lives of its students by helping them secure futures in higher education.

Vision Statement: A vision statement is a broad, aspirational statement of what you hope to achieve. It should answer, 'What world do you want to create?

- Example: "To bring drone technology to the masses. Unlocking genius in communities that are typically forgotten."

Mission Statement: A more specific articulation of how you intend to achieve your vision. It should be concise and action-oriented.

- Example: "To develop education tools and training that will foster innovation within underserved communities globally."

Action Step: Write your vision and mission statements. Keep them simple, inspiring, and focused on the core of what you want to change. This is the foundation for your entire plan.

2. Identify the Problem You Want to Solve

Coates identified the problem early on: the band didn't have the discipline or motivation needed to succeed at a competitive level. Moreover, many students were unaware of the scholarship opportunities available through their musical talents. Clearly defining the problem was a crucial step towards him making a lasting impact. Spend time understanding the root causes, effects, and scope of the issue you're passionate about. Knowing this will guide you to create a solution that addresses the real need, not just the symptoms. Brian addressed the shortfalls of the program he inherited by implementing strict discipline, fostering a sense of responsibility among students, and exposing them to performance opportunities that would open doors to scholarships

Research the Problem: Gaining knowledge through reports, discussions with experts, documentaries and other forms will make you more credible and help you see more clearly ways to help.

- Example: If your passion is fighting climate change, ask: What specific part of climate change are you focusing on? Deforestation? Carbon emissions? Waste reduction?

Narrow Your Focus: While you may feel the pull to solve many issues at once, focus on one specific aspect where you can make the most difference. Then start small with that aspect.

- Example: "Reducing plastic waste in the ocean by creating biodegradable packaging solutions."

Action Step: Write a clear problem statement. Specify the issue, its scope, and why it matters to you and the world. Keep it focused and based on your research.

3. Set Clear, Achievable Goals

The goals in your plan should be **S**pecific, **M**easurable, **A**chievable, **R**elevant, and **T**ime-Bound (SMART). Mr. Coates plan set clear, achievable goals. He aimed to expose students to scholarship opportunities and guide them toward earning multiple offers. In 2023, he proudly watched as six of his students signed scholarship offers, collectively earning $2.5 million. By 2024, that number had more than doubled, with 11 students securing over $5.5 million in scholarship offers.

Short-term Goals: Milestones that give you wins for the near future (weeks to months).

- Example: "Partner with local businesses to distribute 1,000 biodegradable packaging solutions within six months."

Long-term Goals: These are the broader, larger outcomes you want to see over the next few years.

- Example: "Reduce plastic waste in the Pacific Ocean by 10% over the next five years through nationwide adoption of sustainable packaging."

Action Step: Define at least 3 short-term and 3 long-term goals that will help you track progress and keep you on course.

4. Develop a Detailed Action Plan

If you are not a person who is used to being detailed this is where your team may be of us. It's time to create actionable step-by-step guides to achieve milestones and goals. Each action step should be specific and connected to the goals you've set. Let this serve as the GPS directions from point to point.

For Mr. Coates, his detailed plan included exposing students to scholarship opportunities, preparing them for competitions, and helping them navigate the college application process. Some of the step-by-step actions were sending students to competitions like the Southern Heritage Classic, connecting them with resources and contacts who are empowered to award band scholarships.

Action Steps: Break down each goal into actionable tasks.

- Example: For the goal of distributing 1,000 biodegradable packages:

1. Research suppliers of biodegradable materials.
    2. Develop prototype packaging with your team.
    3. Partner with a manufacturer for production.
    4. Pitch to local businesses to test the product.
    5. Monitor the product's impact and collect feedback.

Assign Roles and Responsibilities: For each task, assign it to a team member or partner who is best suited to complete it.

- Example: "Research suppliers – Sarah; Prototype development – John; Business outreach – You."

Set Deadlines: Every task should have a clear deadline to ensure steady progress.

- Example: "Complete research on suppliers by October 1st of current year"

Action Step: Create a timeline with specific action steps, who is responsible for each, and when they need to be completed.

5. Identify Resources Needed

To bring your plan to life, you'll need resources. Brian utilized mentors like Dr. Reginal McDonald from Tennessee State University to help his students gain exposure to scholarship opportunities. He also ensured his students had the support they needed to pursue higher education in general. Resources can come in many forms such as financial, human, and technological. Identify what you'll need and how to secure capitals in whatever form you can obtain.

Financial Resources: Estimate the costs for achieving each of your goals (e.g., material costs, marketing, travel). Explore sources of funding such as donations, grants, investors, or crowdfunding.

- Example: "$5,000 for prototype development, $10,000 for initial production."

Human Resources: Identify who you need to help you achieve your goals. This could be volunteers, staff, partners, or advisors.

- Example: "A packaging designer, a marketing expert, and local business partners."

Technological Resources: Determine what tools or technologies you'll need to scale your mission. This could be software, manufacturing equipment, or digital platforms.

- Example: "Biodegradable materials production tools, a project management platform."

Action Step: Create a resource list that outlines the specific tools, funding, and people you need. Research ways to access those resources, whether through networking, fundraising, or partnerships.

6. Anticipate Challenges and Develop Contingency Plans

Every plan faces challenges. Coates anticipated the challenges his students might face, such as the potential reluctance of colleges to offer scholarships or the limited resources available for the band program. By focusing on discipline and building relationships with colleges, he was able to mitigate these challenges and secure scholarships for his students. What are the potential roadblocks in your path. Prepare possible solutions ahead of time. Use these potential challenges as a motivator and team builder.

Identify Potential Obstacles: Think about what could go wrong and where the plan might fall short.

- Example: "What if businesses are resistant to adopting biodegradable packaging due to higher costs?"

Develop Contingency Plans: For each challenge, develop an alternative strategy to stay on track.

- Example: "Offer a discount on the first order to businesses or find alternative suppliers to reduce production costs."

Action Step: Make a list of potential risks and develop backup plans for each scenario to mitigate their impact. This is a moment for team building. Create some team building exercises around developing the list. It will be a great way for the team to communicate outside of normal operations.

7. Measure Success and Adapt Along the Way

As you execute your plan, it's essential to monitor your progress and measure success. Coates measured the success of his plan through scholarship offers and competition results. What metrics will show that you're on the right track? . Each year, as more students received scholarships and the band placed higher in competitions, Coates adapted his plan to scale the program further. How will you know if your solution is making a difference? By 2024, the band had earned over $5.5 million in scholarship offers and placed 2nd in a prestigious regional competition. He created an annual program to update the community and provide a year over year report on the impact his program is making. You too should regularly evaluate and adapt as needed.

Set Metrics for Success: Define how you'll measure progress toward your goals. These could be quantitative (e.g., number of products distributed, funds raised) or qualitative (e.g., customer feedback, impact on the community).

- Example: "Distribute 1,000 packages and reduce plastic waste by 20% in participating businesses."

Regular Check-ins: Schedule regular team meetings or reviews to evaluate your progress and make necessary adjustments. If possible turn them into events that can also be used as publicity, motivation and recruitment.

- Example: "Monthly team meetings to assess distribution progress and customer feedback."

Action Step: Create a list of key performance indicators (KPIs) and a schedule for checking in on your progress. Be ready to pivot and adapt your plan as new challenges and opportunities arise.

8. Build a Support Network

Changing the world can't be done alone. Coates built a support network that included mentors, college recruiters, and community members who believed in his vision. Surround yourself with mentors, partners, supporters, and like-minded individuals who share your passion. These people will provide advice, resources, encouragement, and sometimes, new ideas to keep you moving forward. Brian utilized his network to build a support grid that included mentors, college recruiters, and community members who believed in his vision

Find Mentors and Advisors: Seek out people who have experience in your field or who have successfully achieved similar goals. Their guidance will be invaluable.

- Example: "Reach out to local environmental leaders or entrepreneurs who have launched sustainability initiatives."

Grow Your Network: Attend industry events, join online communities, and network with others who can support your mission.

- Example: "Join sustainability groups, attend environmental conferences, and connect with potential investors."

Action Step: Identify key individuals and groups that can offer support and expertise. Schedule time to meet with mentors or network with potential partners.

Conclusion: Your Plan Is the First Step to Changing the World

Through vision, discipline, and strategic planning, Coates transformed a struggling band program into a powerhouse that changed the lives of its students. The steps outlined in this chapter will set you up to build a solid, actionable plan to make your passion a reality. Remember that world-changing missions don't happen overnight, it took five years for Alcovy High to reach the goal of over a million of dollars of scholarship money for his students.

Remember patience, perseverance, and a willingness to adapt as you learn are the keys to success. Maintain your clear vision, accomplish the actionable goals, and secure the precise support needed. You and on the path to have the power to create real, lasting change.

5

Execute The Plan

Executing a plan, as Coach Jim Vance knows, requires more than sticking to a schedule; it's about commitment, resilience, and the ability to adapt. As a coach, author, and sport technology consultant based in San Diego, Vance uses these traits to guide athletes like 2016 US Olympic triathlete Ben Kanute, among others, to world-class performances. He has developed a 12-week training plan for Olympic triathletes as a reflection of the very principle of his belief in execution.

So here we are at the most crucial step: executing your plan. This is where ideas turn into action, where the hard work and passion meet the real world. Stay focused on the mission, and don't allow the initial momentum to wane. Stick to the plan, but don't be afraid to pivot when necessary. Execution is as much about adaptability as it is about focus.

As a former collegiate track and cross-country athlete at the University of Nebraska, Vance learned early on that discipline and planning are the bedrock of success. His transition to triathlon, where he won two amateur world championships and trained at the Olympic Training Center, only reinforced this belief. It was during this period that Vance honed his understanding of structured training, which later became the backbone of his coaching approach. He achieved top finishes in Ironman racing, including a third-place finish at

Ironman Florida in 2006, demonstrating his ability to not only plan but also to execute those plans under pressure.

Initial Action Step: Begin taking action, no matter how small. Don't wait for the perfect moment—start today. Execute your tasks one by one, meeting your milestones and adjusting as needed.

Here are some of the best ways to effectively execute the plan you've just developed for changing the world:

1. Break the Plan Into Actionable Steps

Mr. Vance took a grand goal and broke it down into steps. He then took those steps and broke them down into daily and weekly tasks. Developing clear goals that can be put into action immediately helps keep a team focused and prevents them from being overwhelmed. For week 1 in his 12-week training model athletes undergo easy swims, Functional Threshold Power (FTP) bike tests, and progressive run intervals, each with clear objectives.

Daily/Weekly Task Lists: Create detailed to-do lists with clear deliverables, deadlines, and who is responsible for each task.

- Example: "This week: Contact three potential suppliers, draft the first version of the website, and create a marketing plan."

Action Step: Turn your long-term milestones into bite-sized, specific tasks with deadlines, and assign them to the appropriate team members.

2. Ensure Accountability and Clear Roles

Vance ensures that each training phase has clear goals. He tracks athletes' progress using data-driven tools that monitor key metrics such as heart rate and power output. Execution requires accountability. Each team member needs to know exactly what they are liable for and how their performance impacts to the bigger goal. Empower people to have ownership of their tasks and regular check-ins to track progress.

This emphasizes the importance of accountability, both for the coach and the athlete, much like the execution process outlined in the book(Jim Vance is an elite e...).

Set Up Accountability Systems: Use tools like project management software (e.g., Asana, Trello) to assign tasks, track progress, and ensure transparency.

- Example: "John is responsible for securing funding; Sarah will lead the marketing campaign. Weekly team meetings will review progress."

Action Step: Assign clear roles and responsibilities for each part of the plan and establish accountability check-ins or reports to monitor progress.

3. Build a Team Culture of Execution

The culture within your team can make or break the success of your plan. Vance builds a culture of execution by encouraging both proactivity and problem-solving. Ensuring his athletes have backup strategies for unexpected hurdles. For example, Vance's athletes are encouraged to adapt quickly if injuries or fatigue occur during training. This fosters an execution-focused mindset by encouraging commitment, proactivity, and problem-solving. Work to make sure your team is united on the value of pushing forward, taking initiative, and resolving problems as they happen.

Promote Proactivity: Encourage your team to take initiative and solve challenges without waiting for instructions.

- Example: "If a supplier falls through, have a list of backup options ready and act quickly to replace them."

Focus on Solutions, Not Problems: When obstacles arise, train the team to focus on finding solutions rather than dwelling on setbacks.

Action Step: Hold a kickoff meeting to set the tone for execution. Emphasize the importance of action, initiative, and maintaining momentum, and celebrate small wins to build a culture of progress. One could also create a reward program around solving problems and execution.

4. Create a Timeline with Key Milestones

Without the proper structure of a timeline; delays, lack of urgency, and unclear progress can creep in. Vance's training schedules are meticulously planned with weekly milestones, progressively intensifying as the race approaches. In week 5 of one of his plans, workouts become more demanding, concentrating on building aerobic endurance and race tempo. Timelines with key milestones make certain that progress is followed, and modifications can be made as necessary to keep the team on target.

Set Milestones: These should be points where critical parts of your plan are achieved (e.g., product launch, fundraising targets, partnerships secured).

- Example: "By month two, we should have developed the prototype. By month six, we need to have raised $50,000 in seed funding."

Track Milestone Progress: Use visual tools like Gantt charts or project management dashboards to track the team's progress and deadlines in real-time.

Action Step: Develop a detailed project timeline with specific deadlines for each task and milestone. Review and update it regularly based on progress.

5. Communicate Effectively and Frequently

Vance's success as a coach relies heavily on open communication with his athletes . Strong communication is essential for keeping everyone on the same page. Regular feedback allows for quick adjustments and fine-tuning; empowering all parties involved. Good communication is a tool for solving issues quickly, and ensuring no one feels disconnected from the mission. Make sure communication channels are clear and accessible.

Regular Team Check-ins: Hold weekly or biweekly meetings to review progress, address challenges, and discuss the next steps.

- Example: "Every Monday, we'll have a 30-minute call to review last week's progress and set priorities for the upcoming week."

Use Communication Tools: Use platforms like Slack, Microsoft Teams, or email to ensure team members are constantly updated on important changes or developments.

Action Step: Set up regular team meetings or status updates. Keep communication open, sharp, and create clear channels for feedback and problem-solving.

6. Remain Flexible and Adapt to Challenges

As Mike Tyson said so eloquently; "Everyone has a plan until they get punched in the mouth." No plan survives unchanged once you start executing it. Obstructions will appear, and some strategies may not perform as projected. To pivot, adjust, and re-strategize without losing sight of your overall mission is a necessary skill for every team.

Embrace Change: Stay adaptable and open to new information. If a part of your plan isn't working, don't hesitate to make necessary adjustments.

- Example: "If the target market isn't responding to your product, consider a marketing shift or explore a new audience."

Learn from Failures: Resilience and wisdom are often fruit grown from the tree of failure. Learning from mistakes is a crucial part of growth. Take time to reflect and make progress. Analyzing what went wrong helps us acquire insights that aid us in making better decisions in the future.

Action Step: Periodically review your plan's progress and outcomes. Be ready to adjust timelines, pivot strategies, or even rethink some aspects of your plan when faced with new realities.

7. Leverage Technology and Tools for Efficiency

Need to know your sleep patterns, or maybe you want to receive personalized data on your performance. Vance leverages technology such as power meters and heart rate monitors to optimize training efficiency and monitor athletes' performance. Tools that modernize work processes, mechanize repetitive tasks, and help manage resources effectively have become a more common part of life. Take advantage of the tools that free up your team to focus on high-impact work.

Use Project Management Tools: Tools like Monday.com, Notion, or Trello help you track tasks, manage timelines, and visualize progress.

Automate Where Possible: Automate tasks such as email marketing, data entry, and social media posting to save time.

Action Step: Identify and implement the right tools for your team. Make sure everyone is trained on how to use them efficiently.

8. Monitor Key Performance Indicators (KPIs)

Continuous evaluation of KPIs ensures tasks are aligned with overall objectives. KPIs are specific metrics that show whether your plan is delivering the desired outcomes. Utilizing quantifiable data help you organize, assess performance and spot areas that may need improvement. By regularly monitoring KPIs, leaders can make informed decisions and adjust strategies in real time

Set Measurable KPIs: KPIs can be as diverse as your mission. Make sure metrics measure actions that push you to your overall mission such as revenue raised, customer engagement, product adoption, or social impact.

- Example: "Track how many new users signed up for the app in the first quarter, how much money was raised in a fundraising campaign, or the amount of waste reduced."

Adjust Based on Results: If you're not hitting key metrics, reassess the tactics and pivot where necessary to better align with your goals.

Action Step: Identify the key metrics that will indicate success and set up a system for regularly tracking and reviewing these metrics.

9. Maintain Focus on the Big Picture

While Vance emphasizes daily execution, he never loses sight of the athletes' ultimate goal: race day. Maintaining this balance of short-term execution with long-term vision keeps athletes motivated. While executing, it's easy to get bogged down in day-to-day details and lose sight of the overarching vision. Periodically take a step back to ensure you're still aligned with the long-term mission and that the daily actions are contributing to it.

Reconnect with the Mission: Regularly remind your team of the ultimate goal and why their efforts matter.

- Example: "At the end of each month, hold a mission-focused meeting to revisit the vision, celebrate successes, and make sure the team stays aligned with the larger purpose."

Avoid Getting Stuck in the Weeds: Delegate smaller tasks to free yourself up for big-picture decision-making and leadership.

Action Step: Schedule regular vision alignment sessions. Take time to reflect on how far you've come, what you've learned, and where you're headed.

10. Celebrate Small Wins and Build Momentum

In his coaching, Jim Vance celebrates athletes' progress, using each small victory to build momentum toward the ultimate goal. Change takes time, and it's important to celebrate the small victories along the way. Acknowledging achievements keeps morale high, builds momentum, and motivates your team to keep pushing toward the goal.

Recognize Successes: Completion of any milestone is an opportunity to celebrate. Does's matter if its finally getting and interview you needed, launching a new product, securing a key partnership, or hitting a fundraising target.

- Example: "After raising the first $10,000, throw a small team celebration to keep spirits high."

Maintain Team Morale: Keep team energy up by regularly acknowledging individual contributions, publicly recognizing efforts, and offering positive feedback.

Action Step: Create a system for celebrating small wins. This could be a monthly "team win" report, a shout-out on social media, or an internal reward system for meeting targets. As stated earlier remember the individual touch such as handwritten letters and personal gifts help build loyalty to the mission and to you.

Conclusion: Execution Is About Consistency and Adaptability

In conclusion, executing a world-changing plan requires a disciplined approach, adaptability, and consistent focus on both short-term and long-term goals. Jim Vance's journey as a coach, alongside his detailed training methods, provides an exemplary blueprint for how these principles can lead to success, not just in sports, but in any world-changing endeavor. Break down your plan into manageable tasks, foster a culture of accountability and execution, and keep communication lines open. Monitor your progress, celebrate successes, and stay focused on your mission. With persistence, agility, and consistent effort, your plan can lead to real-world impact and create the change you're passionate about.

6

Build on Plan's Successes While Fixing Faults

As you execute your plan, there will be successes and setbacks. Keep track of all successes and setbacks. We should celebrate every win, no matter how minor, because they all signify progress. But equally important is identifying the faults and areas that need improvement. When the plan has been executed go back and look through those successes while reevaluating the setbacks.

The ability to learn from both successes and setbacks is key to refining your work and driving continuous improvement. The stories of the Blue Angels and various lessons from the military's After Action Review (AAR) system exemplify this approach and offer invaluable insights into how organizations can succeed by iterating on both wins and failures.

Action Step: After each major milestone and the end of the overall plan, review your progress. What worked well? What didn't? How can you optimize your approach moving forward? Make necessary adjustments and move on.

Building on an executed plan's successes while fixing its faults is a critical part of continuous improvement. It allows you to maximize what's working, address challenges, and adapt for long-term sustainability. Here's how you can do it effectively:

1. Evaluate Results Thoroughly

Once you've executed your plan, the first step is to evaluate what worked and what didn't. Conduct a detailed review of the outcomes to understand the successes and identify the areas that fell short. Each member of the Blue Angels team answers three questions at the end of every show: What happened? Why did it happen? What will we do differently next time?". This evaluation process is disciplined and involves all team members, ensuring a comprehensive understanding of both successes and near-misses.

Success Metrics: What key performance indicators (KPIs) were met or exceeded? What specific strategies led to these successes?

- Example: "We exceeded our goal of raising $50,000 within six months due to our successful crowdfunding campaign."

Identify Faults: Where did the plan fail to meet expectations? What were the major challenges, delays, or obstacles?

- Example: "Our outreach efforts to large corporations didn't yield as many partnerships as expected."

Action Step: Conduct a post-execution review meeting with your team. List the key successes and failures and gather feedback from all involved. This will provide a comprehensive view of both strengths and weaknesses.

2. Leverage the Successes

One of the lessons shared by the Blue Angels is the importance of *reinforcing what went well*. Build momentum from what worked by doubling down on those strategies, scaling successful initiatives, and applying similar principles to other areas of the project. Even when things go right, there is room to improve and elevate the standard. In one of their debriefs, a pilot shared that after a successful maneuver, they still discussed how to execute it even better next time. This level of refinement is what makes their performances so consistent and world-class(Chapter 6 notes).

Scale What Works: If a particular approach or strategy was effective, look for ways to scale it up or replicate it in other areas.

- Example: "Our social media campaign brought in many small donors. We can scale this approach by investing more in targeted ads and expanding to other platforms."

Expand Your Reach: Use successful outcomes as a launchpad for new opportunities, such as leveraging achievements to gain additional support, attract new partnerships, or secure more funding.

- Example: "Our fundraising success will help build credibility when approaching major investors."

Action Step: Identify 2-3 key strategies or tactics that worked well and brainstorm ways to scale or replicate them for broader impact.

3. Analyze the Root Causes of Failures

The AAR system, which is widely used across military operations, focuses not only on identifying mistakes but also on finding the root causes behind them. When things don't go as planned, it's essential to dive deep into the root causes. Surface-level fixes won't address underlying issues (Chapter 6 notes). This is crucial because it prevents repeating the same mistakes in the future. Similarly, when Bill Belichick was the coach of the New England Patriots, he conducted post-game "autopsies," where he dissects both wins and losses equally to learn from them(Chapter 6 notes).

Root Cause Analysis: Ask the *why* of what went wrong. Focus on resolving any issues with team communication, misaligned goals, inadequate resources, or external factors.

- Example: "Our corporate outreach was ineffective because our value proposition wasn't aligned with what businesses are looking for."

Use Feedback: Don't get feedback from just team members, of possible include partners and stakeholders. A diversity of insights can shed light on concerns that might not be immediately evident.

- Example: "Our volunteers mentioned they felt undertrained, leading to slower progress in certain areas."

Action Step: Perform a root cause analysis for each fault you identify. Break down the contributing factors and determine if the issue stems from strategy, execution, resources, or external variables.

4. Develop Actionable Solutions for Faults

In high-performing teams, the process of reviewing and fixing faults is not just theoretical. The Blue Angels, for instance, turn their lessons into actionable obligations. Each pilot takes accountability for their mistakes and outlines a clear path for immediate improvement(Chapter 6 notes). This culture of accountability ensures continuous progress. The goal is to fix the immediate issues and put systems in place to prevent them from recurring.

Create Improvement Plans: Develop a clear, actionable plan for each issue, outlining steps for resolution and setting a timeline for implementation..

- Example: "To fix the corporate outreach issue, we will revise our value proposition and focus on businesses that align with our sustainability mission. We'll test this new approach within the next two months."

Assign Ownership: Assign responsibility for fixing the issue to specific team members. However as the leader you will fail if you don't ensure the responsible person does not have the resources and support needed to implement changes.

- Example: "Sarah will lead the revised outreach strategy and will be responsible for securing 3 new corporate partnerships in the next quarter."

Action Step: Create a fault-fixing roadmap. For each identified fault, specify the corrective actions, responsible team members, and timelines.

5. Adapt and Iterate

Adaptation is central to both the military's and the Blue Angels' success. Flexibility and adaptation are key to building on successes and fixing faults. The Blue Angels adjust to new environments, such as different wind speeds or altitudes at various airshows, and modify their plans accordingly(Chapter 6 notes). This flexibility ensures that they can perform consistently no matter the external conditions. As you implement solutions, be prepared to continuously iterate and improve. Execution isn't fixed; it's a cycle of understanding and improving.

Test New Approaches: After implementing fixes, monitor how they work in practice. If they show signs of improvement, build on them. If not, be willing to iterate further.

- Example: "We'll test the new corporate outreach strategy by targeting a small group of businesses first and then expand based on feedback and results."

Learn and Refine: World-changing efforts often evolve over time. Remain open to new methods, emerging technologies, or strategies that may make your original plan more effective.

- Example: "By incorporating feedback, we'll refine our product offerings based on customer needs we hadn't considered during the initial launch."

Action Step: Set up a system for continuous feedback and iteration. Regularly review the success of new solutions and be prepared to adjust your approach based on what you learn.

6. Celebrate and Communicate Successes

The Blue Angels don't just fix what went wrong—they also celebrate what went right. As you build on successes, it's essential to acknowledge and celebrate them, both internally and externally. Every member gets a chance to share what they executed well, reinforcing the positive aspects of their performance (Chapter 6 notes). This boosts morale, motivates the team, and can also attract additional support. Celebrating these wins encourages the team and hardens a culture of excellence.

Celebrate Internally: Recognizing team efforts and individual contributions keeps morale high and reinforces a culture of progress.

- Example: "We'll celebrate achieving our fundraising goal by recognizing key contributors during our next team meeting."

Share Success Externally: Publicizing your achievements helps you build credibility, attract new supporters, and gain momentum for future efforts.

- Example: "We'll send out a press release and update our social media channels with the news of our successful pilot program."

Action Step: Create a communication plan for sharing successes both internally (with the team) and externally (with stakeholders, funders, and the public).

7. Incorporate Learnings Into Future Plans

As state earlier the military incorporates learning into future plans through a process known as after-action reviews. By methodically applying these object lessons, the military enhances operational effectiveness and adapts strategies for potential battles. This continuous learning process strengthens preparedness and ensures overall mission success.

Integrate Feedback: Use what you've learned to refine your long-term strategy. Adjust your approach based on what worked and what didn't.

- Example: "We'll integrate our successful crowdfunding tactics into all future fundraising campaigns, while refining our outreach based on feedback."

Improve Systems and Processes: If certain internal systems (like communication, decision-making, or workflow) proved to be inefficient, improve or automate them for future initiatives.

- Example: "We'll streamline project management using a new tool to ensure better collaboration and task tracking across teams."

Action Step: After reflecting on your successes and failures, update your long-term strategy, systems, and processes to incorporate what you've learned.

8. Engage Stakeholders for Long-Term Support

Trust is key in any long-term relationship. Each stakeholder needs to trust you are doing your best on your quest to change the world. Long-term stakeholders are crucial for sustained success. Create opportunities for them to get involved and always keep them updated. Engaging stakeholders ensures sustained support and buy-in as you move forward.

Report Back: Regularly update your stakeholders on your progress. Use your wins as proof of your effectiveness and demonstrate how you're addressing challenges.

- Example: "We'll send quarterly reports to funders showing how their contributions helped achieve specific goals, along with how we are addressing any setbacks."

Engage New Supporters: Highlighting your successes, particularly after fixing faults, can help bring in new investors, partners, or volunteers.

- Example: "We'll use the results of our pilot program to apply for larger grants and approach new partners for scaling."

Action Step: Create a stakeholder engagement plan that includes regular updates, success stories, and transparency around challenges and how you're fixing them.

Conclusion: Success Is Built Through Reflection, Adaptation, and Growth

Both the Blue Angels and the military's After Action Review system demonstrate that building on success while fixing faults is crucial for long-term success. In your journey to change the world, this iterative process of celebrating victories and learning from mistakes will keep your organization dynamic, adaptable, and always moving forward. By evaluating outcomes, addressing weaknesses, and reinforcing strengths, you will continuously improve and achieve greater heights. Consistent adaptation and iteration ensure that your plan continues to evolve and grow, allowing you to create lasting change in the world.

7

Do It All Over Again!

The work of changing the world is never done. This is where we embrace the importance of continuous progress, building on successes while setting new goals. Michael V. Roberts' story, perfectly embodies this principle. Starting in the 1970s with a small consulting firm, Roberts and his brother built a business empire spanning real estate, telecommunications, and broadcasting. Each success became the foundation for the next, and Roberts never stopped refining his approach. From revitalizing his childhood neighborhood to launching telecommunications ventures, Roberts epitomized the mindset of scaling success while fixing faults. The cycle of plan, execute, review, and improve is ongoing. Each iteration brings you closer to your goal and creates even more ripple effects in the world.

Action Step: Take the lessons from your successes and failures, and apply them to the next phase of your mission. Keep moving forward with renewed passion and a sharpened focus.

The process of changing the world is cyclical, and once you've gone through the initial stages—building a team, evaluating weaknesses, creating and executing a plan, and refining it—you can start the process all over again with more insight, experience, and momentum. Here's the best way to restart the process and continue evolving your mission:

1. Reignite Your Passion with a Refined Vision

After your first cycle of action, your understanding of your passion and mission will likely be deeper. This was true for Michael Roberts who's passion evolved with every milestone. Let your experience enhance your vision for the next level. Mr. Roberts's early vision of supporting minority businesses expanded to owning over 30 companies across diverse industries. At this step, reflect on the lessons you've learned, re-examine the reach of your mission, and reignite the core passion that started it all. Michael's passion was reignited by his desire to create lasting community impact, evident in his redevelopment projects in St. Louis. Projects like Roberts Brothers Properties, which renovated decaying urban areas, show how his vision constantly grew from business to societal transformation.

Expand or Refocus Your Mission: Now that you've learned from both successes and failures, ask yourself if your mission needs to be adjusted. Should you aim for a broader impact, or perhaps refine your focus to a specific niche where you can be even more effective?

- Example: "We've successfully reduced plastic waste in local communities. Next, let's tackle large-scale corporate waste management policies."

Action Step: Host a visioning session with your core team to reassess and expand your mission based on the progress made. Set new, inspiring goals that reflect your renewed focus and experiences.

2. Recruit Fresh Talent and Strengthen the Team

Your initial team has achieved great things, but you've probably identified new gaps, additional expertise needed, or areas where fresh energy could help. Throughout his career, Roberts continuously expanded his team, involving family members, expert business partners, and mentors. Strengthen your team by bringing in new members with complementary skills or perspectives, while continuing to support and develop your existing team. While his brother remained in a pivotal role, Mr. Roberts made sure his children also contributed to the businesses. This shows how important it is to keep strengthening your team with fresh talent while nurturing existing relationships.

Fill Newly Identified Gaps: As you grow, you may need specialists who weren't necessary in the early stages, such as legal experts, financial advisors, or marketing professionals.

- Example: "We succeeded at the grassroots level, but now we need a seasoned policy advocate to help scale our efforts to a national level."

Keep Existing Team Motivated: Provide opportunities for current team members to grow, learn new skills, and take on leadership roles in the next phase.

- Example: "Our project manager can now take on a more strategic role, overseeing larger projects as we scale."

Action Step: Conduct a team evaluation and create a recruitment plan for new talent. At the same time, hold growth-focused conversations with current team members to ensure they remain aligned and motivated.

3. Develop a New, Ambitious Plan Based on Insights

Yes, we need to back to Step 3 with a better understanding of what works and where challenges lie, creating a more refined and ambitious plan. This plan should take your mission to the next level, using the lessons learned from your first cycle to evade past errors and benefit from strengths. After the success of their consulting business, Roberts and his brother expanded into broadcasting, wireless communications, and real estate. Their confidence in entering new industries illustrates how building on early wins can lead to even bigger achievements. Every new venture was based on lessons learned from the past, whether that was creating Roberts Broadcasting or Roberts Wireless Communications.

Incorporate Feedback: Use the insights gathered from the previous plan's execution to build a more robust strategy, accounting for previously identified risks and opportunities.

- Example: "We learned that small businesses are quicker to adopt our solutions, so our new plan will target small business coalitions first, before moving to larger corporations."

Set More Scalable Goals: If you feel like you are ready build on the successes you've achieved and start to scale up. Setting more ambitious goals while making sure they are achievable goals, so you don't stop the momentum you have created.

- Example: "We've reduced plastic waste in five cities. Now, let's expand our efforts to 50 cities over the next three years."

Action Step: Assemble your team to create a new plan, ensuring it is both actionable and ambitious. Set clear milestones and metrics for success, based on what you've learned.

4. Reignite Momentum and Resources

After the first cycle of change, you've likely developed a stronger network and a clearer understanding of how to mobilize resources. Use this to reignite momentum, securing more funding, support, and partnerships to tackle the next stage of your mission. Roberts consistently leveraged his successes to attract new opportunities and resources. His transition into wireless communications in the late 1990s required a $78 million investment, which he secured by building on his existing business reputation and relationships.

This is a clear example of how past accomplishments can serve as leverage for larger, future ventures.

Leverage Previous Successes: Use the results and impact from your first plan to attract new stakeholders, funders, and partners.

- Example: "We'll present our successful case studies to larger foundations to secure
- grants for expansion."

Expand Your Resource Base: Identify new funding sources, partnerships, and technological tools that will help you scale your mission more effectively.

- Example: "We'll partner with an environmental tech firm to scale our waste-tracking technology to a global level."

Action Step: Create a fundraising and partnership strategy that highlights your initial success and shows a clear path for even greater impact. Use your growing credibility to bring in new resources.

5. Continue to Refine Execution and Adaptability

The next stage of execution should be even more streamlined. Having learned from previous mistakes, you can implement a more efficient execution plan with better processes, improved communication, and tighter project management. Roberts' ability to pivot across industries—from consulting to broadcasting and then wireless communications—demonstrates his commitment to refining execution with every step. For instance, when he launched WRBU-TV, he introduced innovative automated systems to streamline operations(Michael Roberts. His adaptability allowed him to succeed in multiple business arenas, always improving on previous processes.

Streamline Operations: As you scale, focus on making your operations more efficient, whether that's through automation, better project management tools, or clearer communication structures.

- Example: "We'll adopt new software to manage multi-city projects simultaneously, improving coordination and reporting."

Improve Adaptability: As you learned in the first round, flexibility is crucial. Build an adaptive strategy that allows for quick changes when obstacles arise.

- Example: "We'll implement regular feedback loops with stakeholders and frontline teams to make real-time adjustments to our plans."

Action Step: Create an improved execution framework that incorporates lessons from the past cycle, focusing on efficiency, flexibility, and strong communication.

6. Focus on Building a Lasting Impact

The next cycle of action should focus not only on expanding your reach but also on building systems and processes that create long-term, sustainable impact. This is where you transition from short-term wins to lasting change. Roberts' long-term focus on real estate redevelopment in his childhood neighborhood and the creation of sustainable businesses shows his commitment to leaving a lasting legacy. By investing in both economic growth and community revitalization, he ensured that his work had a lasting positive impact.

Establish Scalable Systems: Ensure that the systems you're using (whether for fundraising, operations, or communications) are designed to grow with you.

- Example: "We'll create a replicable toolkit for other organizations to adopt our waste-reduction program, allowing us to expand faster without handling all the groundwork ourselves."

Create a Legacy of Impact: Think about the broader legacy of your work and how you can ensure that the change you're making will continue after your direct involvement.

- Example: "We'll train local leaders in the cities we've worked in to ensure they can sustain waste reduction efforts independently."

Action Step: Create a sustainability plan for your mission that includes scaling strategies, leadership development, and community involvement to ensure your efforts have a lasting impact.

7. Inspire and Mobilize a Larger Community

As stated earlier, changing the world is not a solo venture. I applaud you for pushing your current team to this level. Your next aim should be on encouraging and marshaling an even larger community. The more people who join your cause, the more powerful your movement becomes. While Michael Roberts enjoys being a sought-after speaker he found a way to expand his footprint. By writing his book, *Action Has No Season*, he has used his success to motivate and mobilize others to pursue their passions and build businesses.

Share Your Story Widely: Use your success stories and personal passion to inspire others to get involved. This could be through public speaking, media campaigns, or social media engagement.

- Example: "We'll create a documentary showcasing the impact of our work to inspire new advocates, volunteers, and partners."

Grow a Global Network: Expand your network to a national or global level by engaging with like-minded organizations, thought leaders, and activists.

- Example: "We'll join international environmental coalitions to share knowledge and resources, multiplying our impact."

Action Step: Develop a communications strategy that focuses on expanding awareness of your cause, building a larger community of supporters, and encouraging others to take action alongside you.

Conclusion: Start the Cycle with Renewed Strength

Michael V. Roberts' story is one of perpetual growth and reinvention. From selling dashikis in college to becoming a pioneer in broadcasting and telecommunications, his journey exemplifies how to continually build on past success while fixing faults. His story aligns perfectly with the concept of "doing it all over again," proving that world-changing efforts are not finite—they are ongoing. Starting the process of changing the world all over again isn't just about repeating what you've done; it's about using everything you've learned to refine, scale, and amplify your impact. With a stronger team, deeper insights, better resources, and an even clearer vision, your next phase will not only build on past successes but also take your mission to new heights. Keep adapting, learning, and moving forward—and the world will continue to change for the better because of your efforts.

You can change the world—100% guaranteed.

8

Conclusion

In conclusion, **The 7 Guaranteed Steps to Change the World** encapsulates a journey that is both personal and universal. My experience at the CDC's Division of Select Agents and Toxins (DSAT) serves as just one example of how these steps can lead to meaningful and lasting impact. Starting with a passion for emergency management, I built a team of advocates, evaluated gaps in our nation's lab security, and created a plan that unified over 300 individual lab response protocols into one cohesive national strategy. That plan not only received approval from the highest level—the President of the United States—but also set the standard for emergency preparedness across multiple nations, safeguarding over two billion people worldwide.

This journey didn't stop with the creation of a plan. The execution phase involved extensive training, conferences, and constant iteration to ensure the plan worked in every corner of the United States. The work received praise from the U.S. Department of Health and Human Services and soon gained international attention, positioning me as a subject matter expert in global emergency management. Each step reinforced the notion that when passion is coupled with clear, actionable steps, the ripple effects can reach far beyond what you initially envision.

The beauty of the seven steps—**find a passion, build a team, evaluate the**

gaps and seams, create a plan, execute the plan, evaluate the ups and downs, and do it all over again—is that they are universal. Whether your goal is to develop a national emergency response plan or start a small initiative in your local community, these steps can guide you.

This book showcases other stories of ordinary people who have followed these steps to do extraordinary things, sometimes without even realizing it. The steps are timeless, adaptable, and accessible to anyone willing to put in the work. My hope is that you will not only understand these steps but also feel inspired to apply them in your own life.

Remember, the journey to change the world is cyclical. You will continuously refine your approach, rebuild your team, and redefine your goals. With each iteration, you will move closer to your vision of making the world a better place. This book is your guide, but the actions you take are what will turn your passion into progress. The world is waiting for your impact.

About the Author

Jae Brown is a visionary leader, speaker, and advocate for global change, known for his passion for empowering individuals to make a difference in the world. With a background in social entrepreneurship and community activism, he has dedicated his life to creating sustainable solutions for pressing social issues. Jae's expertise in leadership development and strategic planning has inspired countless people to take meaningful action. In *The 7 Guaranteed Steps to Change the World*, he offers practical and proven strategies to help readers become agents of positive transformation. Jae's work has been featured in numerous media outlets, and he continues to mentor the next generation of changemakers. He lives by the philosophy that everyone has the power to change the world, one step at a time.

You can connect with me on:
🌐 https://7steps.life